Know your FEELINGS!

LEVEL HEADERS

written by
Beth Cox & Natalie Costa

illustrated by
Vicky Barker

www.bsmall.co.uk

Published by b small publishing ltd. www.bsmall.co.uk © b small publishing ltd. 2020 • 1 2 3 4 5 • ISBN 978-1-912909-40-7
Editorial: Sam Hutchinson   Design and Art direction: Vicky Barker   Printed in China by WKT Co. Ltd.
All rights reserved. No reproduction, copy or transmission of this publication may be made without written permission. No part of this publication may be reproduced, stored in a retrieval system or transmitted in any form or by any means, electronic, mechanical, photocopying, recording or otherwise, without the prior permission of the publisher.
British Library Cataloguing-in-Publication Data. A catalogue record for this book is available from the British Library.

How this book works

This book is full of activities to help you understand your feelings and be a good friend. The activities all build on each other so are designed for you to work through in order, but you can skip some and go back if you want, or dip in and out if you'd rather - there are no rules.

Use the icons to find top tips, useful information, suggestions for taking it further, and details of additional resources.

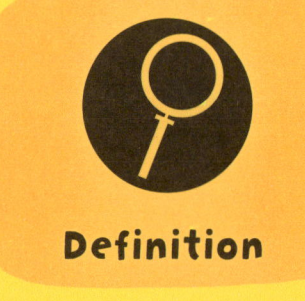

Useful info/fact

Take it further

Top tip

Make your own

Definition

What are your feelings?

Friends and feelings are really closely linked. Your friendships will become stronger when you know and understand your feelings better. Having trusted friends who understand you helps you feel safe and able to express your feelings.

Friendships are not always easy though. You might sometimes feel nervous about making new friends, falling out or having tricky conversations. But every friendship has wobbles, and being able to understand yourself and your feelings, and see things from someone else's point of view, will help you feel empowered and confident. All this will allow you to be the best friend you can be.

Contents

4-5	On your team	20-21	Reasons why
6-7	A good friend	22-23	Talk it out
8-9	Beyond labels	24-25	Magic bubble
10-11	Know yourself	26-27	Every mood has a message
12-13	Making friends	28-29	Sitting with your feelings
14-15	Someone else's shoes	30-31	Get inspired
16-17	Think-feel-act	32	Take it further
18-19	What's the story?		

On your team

Everyone needs a team. You need people around who love and care for you, and whom you can turn to for help. But you also need people who make you laugh, who you can have fun with and who will listen to you. Your ancestors had to be part of a tribe in order to survive, and the human brain is still wired for this kind of connection — you cannot function without it.

Your team might be made up of friends, family, people you live with or a mixture. It could also include people from school, from your hobbies or from your community. Your team should be made up of people who love and support you, who want the best for you and who make you feel good about yourself and realise how great you really are.

Mirror neurons help us feel connected. They are brain cells that activate when you watch someone do something. When you see a person smile, even if you do not smile yourself, the neurons in your brain that you use to smile will fire up.

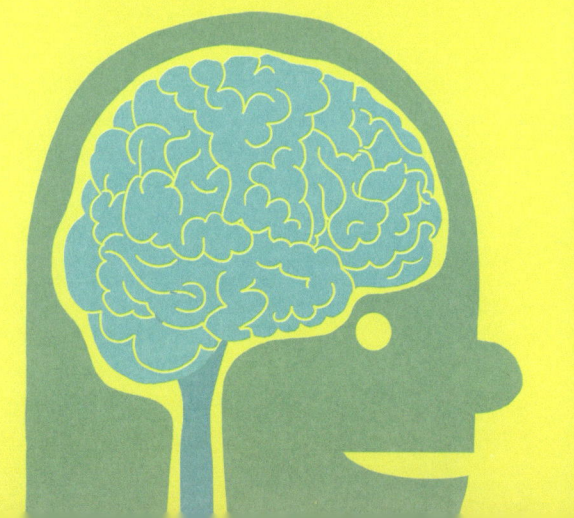

"Human beings are built for connection – it's wired into the depths of our being ... This is why we're the healthiest and happiest when we're connected to a group of people ... "
- Paul Hokemeyer

TEAM _____

Write your name here.

Write the names of the people who are on your team on the 'team bibs'. Make sure you include people in real life, but you can also include a well-known person you admire or someone who promotes a positive message.

Decorate the bibs with things you like to show that this is your team.

Remember that although these people are on your team, you are on their team too. Just as they support you, it is your job to support them too!

A good friend

Look back at the people on your team. I bet they are not all there for the same reasons. Just like with friendships, some friends make you laugh, others are good listeners, and others share similar interests. Of course, some friends might do all these things.

Think about all the different qualities you value in your friends and consider that they might value the same qualities in you. Or there might be other things about you they value. This is what is important and makes you a good friend.

- Funny
- Curious
- Dependable
- Kind
- Determined

"Friends are the family you choose for yourself."
– Unknown

👍 Animals form lifelong friendships with other types of animal. This has been seen in chimpanzees, horses, elephants, bats and dolphins. The animals that had these friendships also had better health.

Choose three people and draw one of them in each square. Think about why you are friends with each of them: Why are they important to you? What makes them a good friend? Why do you value their friendship? Write the answers in the border around each picture.

You do not have to just choose children — you could choose an adult as well.

Draw yourself in this frame and write all the things that make you a good friend in the border. If you are not sure, then you can ask your friends

Beyond labels

Labels are everywhere. Sometimes labels are helpful and sometimes they are the exact opposite. People label others by how they look, what they wear, what they can do or what gender they are. But labels are limiting. They make you focus on one thing about that person and stop you seeing everything else about them. You might also assume some incorrect things.

Someone might have the label 'shy', 'loud' or even 'naughty'. These labels are not who they are, they are just some of their behaviours. There is probably a good reason why they behave that way but that is just one part of them, not all of them.

By looking beyond the labels that are put on things, you can start to see how interesting you and others are. This will help with forging strong friendships.

We can start by looking at the 'labels' we put on objects and how that could limit their use. The yellow lines show the obvious uses and the green lines show the less obvious uses.

- make a card
- write a story
- make a paper aeroplane
- make a list
- keep a diary
- make a paper flower
- journal
- notebook
- make a paper boat
- make a paper hat

⭐ If you just focused on the obvious uses for the notebook, you would have missed out on all the other things that you could use it for.

"People are too complicated to have simple labels."
- Philip Pullman

Think of something that has some obvious uses (or choose from the suggestions below) and brainstorm the obvious uses. Then get creative and think about how else it could be used.

- jug of milk
- bucket of water
- cardboard box
- piece of string
- tote bag

You can do something similar for people you know. Think about what labels you or others might have given them, and then think about how they are so much more than that. Start with a teacher. I bet they are also a coach, a nurse if you feel unwell. Out of school they might be a parent, or like playing a particular sport.

Know yourself

If you only focus on the main qualities that you or others have, then you start to think of people fitting into certain categories. The most common categories used to describe types of people are 'introvert' and 'extrovert'.

These two categories suggest that people are one or the other, when in fact most people are a bit of a mix or feel differently in different situations. These categories are just another way of labelling people. They are a bit like boxes that people get stuck in and cannot escape.

So how do you know who you are? Looking at lots of characteristics can help you see that you are lots of different things and that you cannot easily be put into a box.

Extrovert: An outgoing, socially confident person.

Introvert: A person who prefers calm and places that are not too stimulating.

Think about one of your friends. Look at the list of words and choose which ones apply to them. I bet there are more than you think.

Now look at the words again. Colour in all the ones that apply to you. Can you see how some contradict each other?

- Adventurous
- Big-thinking
- Cooperative
- Courageous
- Determined
- Calm
- Cheerful
- Creative
- Curious
- Energetic
- Confident
- Considerate
- Daring
- Dedicated
- Enthusiastic

Flexible
Fair
Forgiving
Funny
Friendly
Generous
Genuine
Gentle
Hardworking
Honest
Helpful
Imaginative
Leader
Independent
Logical
Observant
Loyal
Optimistic
Patient
Organised
Perceptive
Playful
Realistic
Precise
Proud
Reflective
Relaxed
Reliable
Selfless
Responsible
Sensitive
Shy
Serious
Sociable
Sympathetic
Thoughtful
Tidy
Trusting

> ⭐ Choose three characteristics that you would like to have more of. Set yourself a challenge that will help you achieve this. What one step can you take straightaway?

1. _____

2. _____

3. _____

Making friends

Making friends seems to come easily for some people, but others find it harder. Big changes such as moving house or school can seem daunting because you know you will have to start again at making friends, but as the new person you will have a fresh start and lots to talk about with people.

Perhaps it is even harder to make friends when nothing has changed, as it might feel strange to try and start a friendship with someone you already sort of know.

Things that will make it easier to make friends:

- Ask questions and be interested in what someone has to say.
- Think about what you would want someone to ask or say, if they were talking to you.
- Try to find something you have in common.
- Find something that you do not have in common but want to find out more about. You might learn something new.

"Be genuinely interested in everyone you meet and everyone you meet will be genuinely interested in you."
- Rasheed Ogunlaru

"You can make more friends in two months by becoming interested in other people than you can in two years by trying to get other people interested in you."
- Dale Carnegie

Start by thinking about what qualities you want in a friend. This might help you work out what kind of friend you want to be.

Brainstorm some questions or some talking points.

Try it out! Talk to someone new. Did your questions help or can you think of any changes you want to make?

What kind of friend do I want to be?

Questions to ask/things to talk about:

What happened?

Someone else's shoes

Friendships have ups and downs, and friends fall out with each other sometimes. Understanding why disagreements happen can help you to resolve them. Empathy is the first step in this journey. Empathy can be described as 'putting yourself in someone else's shoes' or trying to see things how they see them.

Everybody sees things differently. The same situation might be seen with excitement or dread depending on the person, but also on how they are feeling that day.

Empathy:
The ability to understand and share the feelings of another.

"If you could put yourself in someone else's shoes, see what they see, hear what they hear, feel what they feel, would you treat them differently?"
- Philipose John

Put yourself in the shoes of each of the characters with thought bubbles. Write a few words or draw something to show how they feel right now. Do they all feel the same? Are they joyful, excited, bored? How do their feelings differ?

Now think about one of your friends. How would they feel in these scenarios? And how would you feel?

15

Think-feel-act

The reason you see situations differently is because of your thoughts. Your thoughts influence your feelings, these influence your actions, and that influences what happens. The good news is that YOU are in charge of your thoughts and you can change them.

Imagine you are going to a party but you do not know if you will know anyone there. Here are some thoughts you might have about it and how that might play out:

THOUGHTS: I don't know anyone and I won't know what to say to people.
↓
FEELINGS: Shy and nervous.
↓
ACTIONS: Avoid eye contact. Closed posture.
↓
RESULT: Struggle to have a good time. Feel even worse.

THOUGHTS: I know people will want to talk to me. I wonder who I might meet?
↓
FEELINGS: Excited about the possibility of meeting new people.
↓
ACTIONS: Smile. Hold head high. Open posture.
↓
RESULT: Have lots of fun and make new friends.

See how changing the thought changed what happened? Even if you cannot change your thoughts that dramatically, you can try making a small change.

If your first thought about the party is 'I won't know anyone and I won't have anyone to talk to,' you could try thinking 'I wonder who will be there?' Instead of feeling shy, you might start to feel curious. This could change everything!

"Your thoughts and feelings lead to your actions and determine the results you get. It all starts with your thoughts."
- Héritier Ndanyuzwe

4. THOUGHTS

1. THOUGHTS

2. Now picture the situation again. How could you have changed your thoughts about it? Imagine you are in a similar situation. Write down a different thought you could have about it, and the feelings, action and result. How is it different?

3. FEELINGS

2. FEELINGS

3. ACTIONS

2. ACTIONS

1. RESULT

4. RESULT

START HERE

1. Think of a situation where you did not get the outcome or results you wanted. Start at the bottom and write what the result was. Now write what actions you took, what feelings caused those actions and what thoughts caused those feelings.

Think of something that you feel nervous about or not quite sure of. Can you change your thoughts about it? Next time you notice yourself feeling a way you do not like, think about what thought is causing that feeling and see if you can change the thought.

17

What's the story?

The human brain makes sense of the world through stories. So when anything happens in your life, your brain makes up a story about it! Since your brain is designed to keep you alive, it focuses on the negative and things that could go wrong as a way of keeping you safe and protected.

Stories are not always true. When something is making you uncomfortable, ask what story you are telling yourself. What could you tell yourself instead? Can you write a more positive story such as one that is based on hope not fear? Remember that story is a thought, so if you change the thought you can change how you feel about the situation.

Use the phrase 'The story I'm telling myself is ...' to show yourself that there are other options.

The story I'm telling myself is that my friend does not like me because they just walked past me this morning without stopping to talk to me.

"The problem with assumptions is that we believe they are the truth."
- Don Miguel Ruiz

Positive versions of the story:

They were worried because they left their homework at home and wanted to tell the teacher.

They were late, so they were rushing.

They'd had an argument at home and did not want to speak to anyone.

Write about or draw a situation where you felt uncomfortable or upset.

Write about the story you were telling yourself that made you feel that way (remember that the story is the thought that influences how you feel).

Now think about what other stories you could have told yourself. What could the other possibilities have been?

★ You can also use this phrase when talking to friends about difficult situations. It is a powerful way of telling someone how you are feeling without accusing them of anything. It can help them to see how something feels from your point of view.

Reasons why

There is always a reason behind how people behave. Just because you sometimes act in anger, this does not make you an angry person. And just because you do not listen sometimes, this does not mean that you are not interested.

There are so many things that can affect how you act: Being worried about something or frustrated because you cannot solve a problem, finding homework hard or getting into trouble with a teacher, hearing bad news, or just feeling tired or unwell.

Think about a time when you acted in a way that was out of character. When you did not act like the friend you would want, or the person you want to be. What was going on that made you act that way?

There are many reasons why you act how you do, which means that there are many reasons why **others** act the way they do. Remembering this can help when you have a friendship wobble, or when the way someone acts makes you feel bad. Think about what might have caused them to act that way.

"You never know what someone is going through. Be kind, always."
- Unknown

Match the actions to the possible reasons.

ACTION

- Snapping at someone.
- Rushing past a friend.
- Wanting to be alone at playtime.
- Not laughing at a joke.
- Saying something mean.
- Not wanting to play football.
- Not sitting with a friend at lunch.
- Not talking to someone.

REASON

- I forgot my PE kit.
- I can't do my fractions homework.
- I was tired because I went to bed late.
- Someone told me off.
- My dog is old and poorly.
- I was worried about a test.
- I thought they didn't want to talk to me.
- I felt sick.

⭐ If you know a friend is having a hard time, why not invent a secret code? This way, you can let each other know that you are okay, even if they are not up for talking. This could be as simple as thumbs up.

Talk it out

Even the best of friends fall out at times. There is nothing unusual about this. But how you deal with it is important. Now that you have looked at things from other people's perspectives, and thought about what might cause them to act unkindly, you can begin to understand why disagreements happen and start to work out how to deal with them.

Think about how you feel when you have had an argument. What would you need from the person you fell out with, in order to start making amends?

> The words you use only tell a very small part of your story. Non-verbal forms of communication including facial expressions, tone of voice, body language and posture tell a lot more about how you are feeling.

> "Friendship requires great communication."
> - St Francis de Sales

- Remember that how you feel about why something happened is a story you are telling yourself – and that you are both probably telling yourselves different stories.

- Step into their shoes and think about things from their point of view.

- You might not agree with their story but understand that their feelings are still valid. Think back to the reasons why people feel or act certain ways.

- Allow the other person to speak and listen to what they have to say.

- Don't accuse or judge.

- Talk about how something made you feel, rather than what someone did.

- Remember that you are in charge of your feelings.

Think about the last time you fell out with a friend. Make an action plan using the ideas above for what you will do if this happens again.

Action plan

Magic bubble

Once you know yourself and understand that everyone is different, you realise that it is not possible for everyone to get on. People have contrasting interests, separate likes and different personalities. It's okay not to get along with someone, or even to not like somebody, as long as you always remember to be kind.

It would be great if everyone remembered this, but unfortunately some people forget. This does not mean that they are unkind people, but only that they are dealing with their thoughts and feelings the best way they know how.

So what can you do if you are on the receiving end of unkind words? Well, just as you are in control of your own thoughts, you can also control what information you let in and what you keep out. Think of it as a 'magic bubble'.

> Pick your favourite colour and imagine your bubble is this colour. Your bubble will only let in helpful things. Anything hurtful or unkind will bounce right back off. Remember though that some things that may hurt at first actually turn out to be helpful if they are constructive comments from people you respect. It is worth letting them in and listening to them.

My magic bubble

Draw yourself inside your magic bubble. Write some of the helpful and kind things people have said to you inside the bubble. Remembering these things will help the bubble to keep out any unkind words.

"One of the most simple techniques to feel good about yourself is not to let in destructive criticism."
- Marisa Peers

Whenever you need to, picture yourself inside your bubble and let anything unhelpful or unkind bounce right off!

Every mood has a message

Every feeling you have sends you a message. Your mood gives you a clue about the thoughts that are causing your feelings, and what to do about them.

The main emotions, such as fear or anger, can be more accurately described by another feeling. For example, being happy might actually be a feeling of joy, excitement, pride or contentment.

By pinpointing the more accurate feeling, you can then work out the message. Joy usually reminds you of what matters, while pride at your achievements sends a message that you can grow through effort. Anger is often a mask for different feelings — so by working out the feeling behind your anger, you can try to work out the message being sent.

> Emotions are signals that move through us. They are our response to how we see the world.

FEAR
- shyness
- anxiety
- feeling lost
- uncertainty
- fright
- panic
- worry

JOY
- excitement
- hope
- contentment
- happiness
- pride
- pleasure
- confidence
- cheer

SADNESS
- grief
- gloom
- defeat
- misery
- disappointment
- frustration
- rejection
- helplessness
- fear
- loneliness

ANGER
- disappointment
- irritation
- annoyance
- overwhelm
- frustration
- rejection
- jealousy
- feeling trapped
- helplessness
- feeling attacked
- tiredness
- shame
- fear
- loneliness

> Keep a journal of your feelings and emotions over the week. When you feel something strongly, make a note of what caused it and try to work out what this is telling you.

FEELING	CAUSE	MESSAGE	NOTES

Once you start to understand your feelings a bit better, you can improve how you deal with things. You might be able to talk to friends or family about your feelings, or find different ways of resolving problems.

Sitting with your feelings

While some emotions might feel negative and others positive, they are all equally important. We cannot have happiness without sadness, or hope without fear. Some feelings are uncomfortable and sometimes we might be able to change them, or at least want to. But often it is valuable to sit with a feeling. Rather than trying to push it away, try to experience it and deal with it.

This is most true of sadness. Sad things happen in life, it is inevitable. While it might not be very pleasant, there are ways of working through it. Trying to ignore the feeling will only make it grow or come out in a different way.

Draw a full picture of you. Think about a feeling that was uncomfortable and label where you felt it in your body.

Draw or write about it.

Now you have moved past that feeling, what can you tell yourself?

Processing a difficult feeling

- Cry — it is a great way of letting everything out.
- Move your body or do some exercise.
- Talk to someone you trust.
- Think back to the last time you felt this way. Did it last?
- Try to think about any happy memories associated with the difficult feeling. Write the memories down on a piece of paper and keep it as a keepsake.
- Draw the feeling and give it a colour.
- Think about what you would tell a friend who felt this way.
- Take a deep belly breath and imagine breathing out your uncomfortable feeling.

"There are moments when I wish I could roll back the clock and take all the sadness away, but I have the feeling that if I did, the joy would be gone as well."
– Nicholas Sparks

Get inspired

It is easy to look at other people and compare yourself to them. You might want things that they have, or to be able to do things that they can do. But constantly measuring yourself against others and feeling like you are not good enough can make you feel bad about yourself.

Using these feelings as inspiration can be a good thing though. Think about whom you compare yourself to and remember that their skills have not come naturally — they have taken hard work and practice. So use this as your motivation to work hard for the things you want.

And remember, people are probably looking at something that you can do well and wishing that they could do it too.

I wish I could be more like him – he's so good at swimming.

"Don't compare your beginning to someone else's middle."
- Jon Acuff

I wish I could be more like her, she finds it so easy to make friends.

Think of somebody that you compare yourself to. What are they good at that you would like to be able to do?

I want to be good at: ....

Me

Them

1. Make a list of all the things that you can do to help you achieve this.

2. Now make a list of all the things that they do already to help them achieve this.

3. You will probably find that there are more similarities than you thought. Now look at the skills you do not have YET. Choose one of these to start with and make a plan for how you are going to get better at it — remember to take one small step at a time.

If someone has skills you want to learn, you might also have some skills that they want to learn. Maybe you could exchange skills and learn from each other. You might even make a new friend.

Take it further

Do something kind every day.

Give yourself brain breaks.

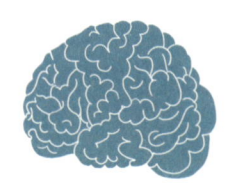

Remember that you are in control of your feelings.

Keep a gratitude journal to help you focus on the positive.

Be yourself!

Try and make a new friend.

Smile!

Be the friend that you want to have.

Speak to people who are on their own.